Communication & Language Program

For Early Years Teachers, Nurseries and Childminders

Published by Early Years Staffroom Limited 2022

Printed in Great Britain © Early Years Staffroom.com Ltd

British Library Cataloguing – in – Publication Data
A catalogue record for this book is available from the British Library

ISBN 978-1-8382048-3-9

All rights reserved. No part of this publication may be reproduced in any form or by any means – graphic, electronic, or mechanical, including photocopying, recording, taping or information storage or retrieval systems – without the prior permission in writing from the publishers.

www.earlyyearsstaffroom.com

Week 1

Monday · Nature Walk	
Resources	Clipboard and pen, blindfolds, access to woodland area
Intent	Develop listening skills, distinguish between different sounds, use a wide range of vocabulary, understand why questions, use longer sentences, represent a point of view, hold a conversation.
Implement	Explain that you will be listening for sounds in a woodland area which is safe. Suggest wearing blind folds to help the ears to listen. Model listening in wonder and ask open questions starting with what, where, how, why, when…for example, Why do you think it makes that sound? Model drawing on the clipboard the pictures of things you think make the sounds you can hear and encourage children to draw pictures if appropriate.
Impact	Can children hear different sounds? Do children answer questions? Can children draw a picture?

Tuesday · Guess the instrument	
Resources	Musical instruments
Intent	Pay attention to more than one thing at a time, develop listening skills, use a wider range of vocabulary, distinguish between sounds.
Implement	Check children know the names of the instruments by saying hello to each instrument. Hide one then describe one of the instruments but do not tell the children it's name. Do you know which instrument makes that sound? Can you make the sound the instrument makes? Children take turns to be the one who describes the instrument if they wish to. Repeat with different instruments. This activity can be done outside in a quiet area as well as inside.
Impact	Can children repeat; hello and instrument names? Can children guess which instrument it might be? Can children attempt to make noises the instruments make? Can children describe an instrument?

Wednesday · Musical statues	
Resources	Music
Intent	Pay attention to more than one thing at a time, develop listening skills, use a wider range of vocabulary, distinguish between sounds, understand why questions, use longer sentences, represent a point of view, hold a conversation.
Implement	Play their favourite music, ask children to clap and dance to the music listening to the beat, when the music stops strike a pose and freeze. The winner is the person who doesn't move. As a variation, ask children to take turns to play the music with instruments. What instrument do you like best and why?
Impact	Do children tell you their favourite music? Can children move/play an instrument to music? Can children take turns?

Thursday · Who is it?	
Resources	Toy

Intent	Develop listening skills, distinguish between different sounds, use a wide range of vocabulary, represent a point of view, hold a conversation.
Implement	In a small group ask one child to sit on a chair with their back to the others. Explain that you are going to give one of the other children a toy and they are to say, "Who is it?" The children must then guess who it is that spoke, then swap.
Impact	Can children attempt to guess who is talking? Can children speak in a clear sentence?
Friday - Duck duck goose	
Resources	None
Intent	Develop listening skills, take turns, develop pronunciation, understand why questions, use longer sentences, represent a point of view, hold a conversation.
Implement	All the players, except the first person who is 'goose', sit in a circle. The first person walks around the circle, tapping each player on the head, saying 'duck' each time until he decides to tap someone and say "goose." That person then becomes the goose and runs after the first person, trying to tag him before he can take his seat. Did you like being the goose? Why/Why not?
Impact	Can children say duck and goose? Can children hear when the goose says goose?

Week 2

Monday · Find the bear	
Resources	Teddy Bear
Intent	Develop listening skills, develop pronunciation, take turns, understand why questions, use longer sentences.
Implement	Take one child aside while a teddy bear is hidden somewhere in the room. Tell the other children they are going to guide the child to the teddy by singing louder as the child gets closer to, or quietly as the child moves further away from the teddy until the child finds the Teddy, taking turns to find the bear. Did you find that easy or hard, why?
Impact	Did children sing high and low to guide the child who was looking for the bear? Do children understand short sentences?

Tuesday · Cup Phones	
Resources	Plastic cups, string
Intent	Develop listening skills, develop pronunciation, understand, and answer questions, use longer sentences.
Implement	Make 'telephones' using cups by creating a hole at the base of each cup and attach a long piece of string securely. Two children can have a conversation with one having the cup on their ear and one child talking into the cup. These can be taken outside so there is plenty of space. Model things that the children might say to each other. Ask the children; Was it easier than you thought it would be to hear your partner? What happened if your string was really long?
Impact	Can children hear each other? Can children talk to each other using correct pronunciation? Can children answer a question?

Wednesday · Giving directions	
Resources	Blindfold, treasure
Intent	Develop listening skills, develop pronunciation, understand, and answer questions, use longer sentences.
Implement	Select one child to be blindfolded (if no one is willing, use a toy instead) then the group needs to take turns to give the child/teddy directions to the treasure (hidden beforehand). For example, Is it under something soft? Is it near the door?
Impact	Can children give directions? Can children understand directions?

Thursday · Giant battleships	
Resources	Large screen for middle of table, large duplo
Intent	Develop listening skills, develop coordination.
Implement	Get a large screen in the middle of the table. On each side put 6 pieces of Duplo with the colours matching each side. One child sits on the other side and one child makes a building. One child goes first and instructs the other what they are doing, for example, I am going to start with the red brick, then I will put the blue brick on top of it etc. When they are finished remove the screen and see if they have a match!

Impact	Can children give instructions? Can children follow instructions?

Friday - A jumbled day	
Resources	None
Intent	To understand how to listen carefully and why listening is important, to learn new vocabulary, take turns, use longer sentences, and describe events in some detail.
Implement	Make deliberate mistakes highlighting to children that sometimes you might get it wrong. Listen carefully to see if I have things in the correct order. Talk about your day, but muddle it all up, for example "At 7 o'clock I woke up and got dressed into my pyjamas, next I went downstairs and had my dinner…etc" Is this correct? What should I have said? Does this make sense? What really happened? Can you tell me about your day so far? Encourage children to take turns and jumble up their day. Can your partner spot any mistakes/correct? Did they listen carefully?
Impact	Can children describe events in some detail? Can children show they have an awareness of how to listen carefully and why listening is important? Can children take turns in conversation?

Week 3

Monday · Jack in a box	
Resources	Smart board or laptop.
Intent	Develop listening skills, develop co-ordination, follow instructions.
Implement	Explain or show a clip of a jack in the box. Ask the children to curl up like Jack in the box. Explain that they can only explode when you call their name. Once exploded they need to stay still like statues until everyone has exploded.
Impact	Can children follow instructions? Can children copy movements? Can children listen and respond to their name?

Tuesday · Song swap	
Resources	Instruments.
Intent	To learn new vocabulary, to recognise rhyme, to listen carefully to rhymes and songs paying attention to how they sound and the changes that occur.
Implement	Take a song or rhyme the children know well and invent new words to suit the children's interests. For example, Mary had a little puppy, a little puppy….'. Use percussion instruments to accompany the new lyrics.
Impact	Can children think of new words? Can children say words that rhyme? Can children spot a word that rhymes?

Wednesday · Talking and walking outside	
Resources	Dictaphone, sound cards in a hat.
Intent	Pay attention to different sounds, use new vocabulary in different contexts, say the initial sound in a word, understand why questions, extend vocabulary.
Implement	Pick a sound out of a hat, take a Dictaphone on a walk and record things that start with that sound, speaking it into the Dictaphone. Ask children open questions about the objects they find, for example, why do you think that was there? I wonder how that got there. Count how many things you found when you return beginning with that sound. You could keep a chart and do this each day.
Impact	Can children find an object that matches the same initial sound? Can children speak the words that they see?

Thursday · Guess the emotion	
Resources	Emotion picture cards.
Intent	Talk about and recognise different emotions, begin to understand emotions and recognise that it is ok to express emotions.
Implement	Turn the pack of emotion cards upside down and start by modelling taking one from the top. Look at the card and act out the emotion, e.g., produce an angry face. What is my emotion? What am I showing? Extend by asking the children Have you ever felt like this before? When did you feel like this? Encourage children to take turns and act out an emotion on the card.

Impact	Can children recognise different emotions? Can children act out different emotions? Can children talk about different emotions?
Friday · Pass the ball	
Resources	Ball (appropriate size).
Intent	To take turns in conversation, to listen and respond appropriately.
Implement	Say a child's name and throw a ball to them to catch it. They then have a turn and say another child's name and then throw it to them. If they are unable to catch it, try rolling the ball instead.
Impact	Can children respond to their name? Can children take turns? Can children listen and respond appropriately?

Week 4

Monday · Teeny tiny nature treasure hunt	
Resources	Empty mini raisin boxes.
Intent	To use a wider range of vocabulary, use language to work out problems and organise thinking and activities, to explain how things work and why they might happen.
Implement	Show children some mini raisin boxes. How many different natural objects can fit into the box? Go on a nature walk outside and collect as many different objects as possible. What did you find? I wonder how many objects can squeeze into the box. Who found the most? Talk about similarities and differences.
Impact	Can children talk in sentences about their findings? Can children talk about similarities and differences?
Tuesday · Shopping bag	
Resources	Shopping bag with a few objects from the home corner.
Intent	To articulate their ideas in well-formed sentences, to develop their listening skills, to understand why listening carefully is important and develop their short-term memory.
Implement	Lay out the objects on the floor and show children your special shopping bag! Play the game 'I went to the shop, and I bought…' using a shopping bag and objects. Each child takes it in turns to select an object and put it into the bag. Each item must be recalled in order. Can you remember what we had put into the bag? What can we do to try to remember?
Impact	Can children remember what was in the bag? Can children speak in a clear sentence?
Wednesday · Sound lotto game	
Resources	Soundtracks game, CD player.
Intent	To listen, discriminate different sounds and extend vocabulary.

Implement	Soundtracks games and farm lotto games are excellent fun to play in small groups and teach children many other skills too. Children love to play games like this and will want to play again and again! What can you hear? What does it sound like? What does the sound remind you of?
Impact	Can children listen carefully? Can children describe what they can hear? Can children distinguish between sounds? Can children use sentences to talk about what they heard?

Thursday · Surprise gift	
Resources	An interesting item wrapped up.
Intent	Develop listening skills, use talk to work out problems and organise thinking and activities, to make predictions.
Implement	Have a pre-made present wrapped up containing an interesting item. Ask the children to predict what might be inside. This could be a nice way to introduce a new resource, or you can pick an item connected to an ongoing theme or story. What do you think might be inside? Why do you think it could be..? What shape does it look like? What does it feel like? Discuss pattern/colour on wrapping paper. Talk about what you like about the wrapped present to open up conversation.
Impact	Can children make predictions? Can children listen to others' ideas? Can children make responses based on good listening?

Friday · Creating a natural den	
Resources	Wood, branches, leaves, twigs, logs, moss.
Intent	Connect one idea or action to another using a range of connectives, to articulate their ideas into well-formed sentences, to use talk to work out problems and organise thinking and activities, to understand why questions.
Implement	Using the available natural materials outside create a den and make it watertight using leaves (and moss if available). What could we use and why? Why do you think that will be a good idea? What will happen if?
Impact	Can children listen to others' ideas? Can children organise their thoughts into well-formed sentences?

Week 5

Monday · What if…?	
Resources	None (unless a picture is used a prompt).
Intent	To express their own views and opinions, to listen to others, to use longer sentences.
Implement	Think up a selection of 'What if..? scenarios, linking them to familiar experiences and stories, such as "What if (the cook) forgot to cook everyone's lunch today?", "What if the Gruffalo joined us for snack time?" Encourage the children to express their views and opinions in response to the 'What if..?' scenario.

Impact	Can children listen carefully? Can children think of their own ideas in response to a question? Can children talk in sentences?

Tuesday - Bubble Fun

Resources	Bubbles, machine if possible.
Intent	To vocalise observations, use new vocabulary, to make comments based on experiences.
Implement	Take the bubbles outside and see if they can be blown fast, slow, high or low, are they big or small? Can we make more? Are there less/fewer?
Impact	Can children respond to their own experiences? Can children understand and respond to simple questions?

Wednesday - Magic Potions

Resources	Small containers, sticks (or spoons), coloured water, mud, natural materials, story book about magic.
Intent	To use imaginative talk, use longer sentences, use new vocabulary.
Implement	Read a book about magic to the children and then explain we are going to make our own potions! Children collect natural items from the outdoors (moss, leaves, daisies, mud etc) and mix with a stick and add coloured water to make a 'magic' potion. Encourage children to talk about their 'magic potion' and what is inside.
Impact	Can children use imaginative talk? Can children use longer sentences? Do children enjoy listening to the story?

Thursday - Shake, rattle and roll

Resources	Scarf.
Intent	To follow an action or instruction, to listen carefully.
Implement	The group stands in a circle outside. Hold a lightweight scarf high up in the air and suggest an action, for example, shake your hands, roll your eyes, jump on the spot, etc. before dropping the scarf; the children do the action until the scarf touches the floor, then freeze.
Impact	Can children follow a simple action, or instruction?

Friday - Making 'bird cake'

Resources	Pinecones, lard, seeds, cheese, raisins, mixing bowl, string, (check for allergies), laminated step by step instructions to refer to.
Intent	To follow simple instructions, to pay attention to more than one thing at a time, to understand a question or instruction.
Implement	Place all the ingredients in a mixing bowl outdoors in the mud kitchen or on a table. Children use their fingers to mix the ingredients together, add an amount of lard according to how much mixture so that it binds together. Squeeze and press the mixture into and around the outside of the cone. Attach a piece of string so it can be hung outside for the birds to enjoy.

Week 6

Monday · Story Circle · Cliffhanger	
Resources	None needed.
Intent	To use a wider range of vocabulary, to take turns in conversation, to use longer sentences, to listen to and add to a story with their own ideas.
Implement	The group stands or sits in the circle and the children take it in turns to contribute one word each to a story begun by you, for example, "Once upon a time, long ago and far away, there lived an enormous...").
Impact	Can children follow a story? Can children make contributions to a story?

Tuesday · Colour Stamp	
Resources	Could have colour cards to assist
Intent	To listen and respond appropriately, to follow instructions.
Implement	The caller calls out a colour and the children stamp around outdoors to touch something of that colour. What did you find?
Impact	Can children follow an instruction? Can children listen and respond appropriately?

Wednesday · The key to my heart	
Resources	Key, music.
Intent	To continue part of a sentence, to use longer sentences, to take turns in conversation, to use a wider range of vocabulary.
Implement	The children sit in a circle and pass a key around to music; when the music stops, the child with the key says, "The key to my heart is..." and names one of their favourite things, for example, ice cream, a person, swimming, favourite story. Adult to model prior to starting.
Impact	Can children talk in a group? Can children use longer sentences? Can children take turns in speaking?

Thursday · Ask a question	
Resources	Ball.
Intent	To listen to and answer a question appropriately.
Implement	Ask a simple question, for example what is your favourite colour? Throw the ball to a child, can they answer the question? Then the child holding the ball asks a question and throws it to who they want to answer.
Impact	Can children listen and respond appropriately to a question? Can children ask questions?

Friday · Tongue twisters	
Resources	None needed.
Intent	To think of ideas and discuss these, to have an awareness of alliteration.
Implement	Give yourself a name with a tongue twister, for example. Silly, special, sunshiny Sam! Help the children to come up with theirs. Use their tongue twister name when calling out their names going forward.
Impact	Can children think of words with the same initial sound as their name?

Week 7

Monday · Colour Kaleidoscope	
Resources	Parachute.
Intent	To listen and respond appropriately, to follow instructions.
Implement	The whole group stand together in a circle holding the parachute outdoors. Everyone is given a colour to remember that they are. Call out a colour name and children who are that colour must swap places whilst the parachute is lifted aloft. Extend to call out two colours at once or even 'kaleidoscope', where everyone goes under, and the parachute is being held up by just the adults.
Impact	Can children follow an instruction? Can children listen and respond appropriately?

Tuesday · The blanket game	
Resources	Blanket.
Intent	To listen carefully in order to discriminate a sound, to imitate different animal sounds.
Implement	Children take turns to go under the blanket and make an animal sound. The rest of the group have to listen carefully to guess the animal. What can you hear? What animal do you think it is?
Impact	Can children listen carefully to guess an animal sound? Can children imitate an animal sound?

Wednesday · I spy · Play 'I spy' with binoculars	
Resources	Binoculars.
Intent	To say a word with the same initial sound, to take turns in conversation, to understand why listening is important.
Implement	Start off by modelling playing I spy, for example, I spy with my little eye something beginning with b. Use binoculars to make it more fun! Give an example then let children have a go. If sounds are too tricky use colours, for example, I spy with my little eye something that is yellow….'.

Impact	Can children say a word that matches the same sound? Can children guess, or attempt to guess, what you spy?
Thursday · Stick tower challenge	
Resources	Sticks.
Intent	To respond to questions, to use talk to organise thoughts and actions, to explain how things work and why they might happen.
Implement	Stack sticks up to see how tall a tower can be built before it falls down. How many do you think we can use? How many did we use? Talk about the size of the sticks.
Impact	Can children use language to make predictions? Can children talk about their tower in longer sentences?
Friday · Woodland crowns	
Resources	Paper, natural materials leaves, petals, moss, glue, tape, scissors.
Intent	To articulate their ideas and thoughts in well-formed sentences.
Implement	Explain to the children we are going to make special crowns. Use a strip of paper or card to measure the child's head prior to them sticking on their natural materials. Once dry, stick the strip together with tape to make a 'crown'. Talk about 'who' they could be, materials used and the design.
Impact	Can children talk about their crown, discussing features and materials? Can children use the language of imaginative role play?

Week 8

Monday · Sounds like	
Resources	Mystery bag, objects from around the room.
Intent	To recognise and say a word with the same initial sound, to take turns in conversation, to understand why listening is important.
Implement	Pass a bag around with some objects for the children to pull out one by one, when someone pulls something out, everyone needs to try to think of something else that starts with that sound.
Impact	Can children say a word that matches the same sound?
Tuesday · Teddy Sleepover	
Resources	Teddy, other objects from around the area.
Intent	To listen carefully, make suggestions, to ask questions to find out more information.
Implement	Pick a teddy for the children to go home with them. Ask the children to help you create a 'sleepover bag' talking about what should go in the bag. Let the children take it in turns to

	have the teddy for a sleepover, and the next day tell everybody what teddy got up to. Encourage the children to listen carefully and ask questions.
Impact	Can children make a suggestion for the sleepover bag? Can children ask a question to find out more information?

Wednesday · Catch a story

Resources	Ball.
Intent	To use a wider range of vocabulary, to take turns in conversation, to use longer sentences, to listen to and add to a story with their own ideas.
Implement	The group stand in the circle and the children take it in turns to contribute one word each to a story begun by you, for example, 'Once upon a time, long ago and far away, there lived an enormous…'. The children take turns by rolling or throwing (depending on what children can do) a ball for someone else to continue the story.
Impact	Can children follow a story? Can children make contributions to a story?

Thursday · Stick and clay animals

Resources	Tuff tray, clay, water in a jug/pot, sticks.
Intent	To use new vocabulary, to use talk to organise themselves and their play, to start a conversation.
Implement	Using materials outside in a tuff tray create animals using sticks for legs, clay for bodies, etc. Children talk about their creations and what the materials represent.
Impact	Can children talk about their clay animal - discussing features and materials? Can children initiate a conversation about their model?

Friday · Hunter, gatherer

Resources	Sticks, wool, moss, grass.
Intent	To use new vocabulary, to use talk to organise themselves and their play, to articulate their thoughts and ideas.
Implement	Children make a nest using natural materials. Have pre-cut pieces of wool (to act as 'worms') hidden around the outdoor area. Children can pretend to be 'birds' and collect the 'worms' to take back to their nests.
Impact	Can children use the language of imaginative role play?

Week 9

Monday · Look at me	
Resources	Mirrors, sound cards, magic bag.
Intent	To copy sounds.
Implement	Give mirrors to the children to look into to observe their faces, lips, teeth and tongue as they make different speech sounds. Pick sound cards out of a bag and say that sound while looking in the mirror, what is happening to your face as you make the different sounds?
Impact	Can children copy a sound?

Tuesday · Mini gardens	
Resources	Paper plates (or boards/trays), natural materials (grass, sticks, petals, daisies, herbs).
Intent	To start a conversation, to use talk to help work out problems and organise thinking and activities and to explain how things work and why they might happen.
Implement	Place objects on a board, plate or tray and make a mini garden. These could just be placed or stuck down with tape or glue. Ask the children about their 'gardens', would you change anything?
Impact	Can children talk about and describe their mini gardens? Can children make suggestions for improvements to their gardens?

Wednesday · What's in the bag?	
Resources	Special bag, objects from around the room, instruments.
Intent	To say a word with the same initial sound, to take turns in conversation, to understand why listening is important, to use new vocabulary.
Implement	You will need a feely bag with some objects inside. Sit the children in a circle and pass the bag around, when you make a noise with an instrument the child holding the bag picks an object, name the object then pass onto the next child to think of something else starting with that sound. Could use partners to help as to not put children on the spot.
Impact	Can children say a word that matches the same sound?

Thursday · Tea and chat	
Resources	'Cafe' table, flowers, cups, plates, tablecloth, teapot, healthy snacks etc, invitations.
Intent	To use new vocabulary in different contexts, to develop social phrases, to start a conversation with an adult or friend and continue it for many turns.
Implement	Provide appropriate drinks in a teapot and healthy snacks. Give out printed invitations for tea and a chat; Dear… please come for tea and a chat, love from…. Help the children give out the invitations to one or two friends. Model the process of hosting a tea party and chatting to guests and encourage the children to linger and converse over their drinks and snacks.

Impact	Can children hold a conversation about something they are interested in? Can children imitate others? Can children take turns in conversations?
Friday · Elf and Fairy homes	
Resources	Small world, natural objects.
Intent	To express a point of view when working with others, to use talk to organise themselves and their play, to use story language and imagination.
Implement	Children create 'homes' for a garden elf or fairy using the natural materials outdoors. Encourage children to work together to make a small group 'home'. Small world characters could be added if they wish, model using story language with the characters.
Impact	Can children listen to others' ideas? Can children express their own views and opinions? Can children use their imagination?

Week 10

Monday · Slow motion	
Resources	None needed.
Intent	To develop listening skills, to respond and copy actions.
Implement	The children stand anywhere in the room or outdoors and respond to the pace of your clapping by walking in time with it, for example. slow claps mean walk slowly, faster claps mean jog.
Impact	Can children make body movements according to the change in pace of sounds?
Tuesday · Changing seats	
Resources	Parachute, different sounds.
Intent	To say a word with the same initial sound, to take turns in conversation, to understand why listening is important.
Implement	Children sit in a circle holding different objects under a parachute. Say to the children they can change seats if they are holding something that starts with a 's' sound etc.
Impact	Can children match the object to the same initial sound?
Wednesday · Snap outdoors	
Resources	Class camera or I-pad, photos.
Intent	To vocalise observations, to ask questions to find out more, to use talk to help work out problems and organise thinking.

Implement	Take part photos of items outdoors and let the children discover where the images have come from. This could be adapted to allow children to do the same for others or the adults. Ask children, how do you know? What can you see? Why do you think it is that?
Impact	Can children talk about their observations? Can children give explanations for their ideas?

Thursday · Draw me a..

Resources	Paper, coloured pencils.
Intent	To give clear instructions, to develop listening skills.
Implement	Working in a small group, begin by asking the children to draw a pink cat, then draw one yourself. Ask one child to suggest another feature for everyone to add, for example, 'please draw two blue spots on the cat', the next child adds another suggestion and so on. Encourage children to listen carefully and follow the instructions so they know what to draw. What do you like best about the cat?
Impact	Can children listen carefully to follow an instruction? Can children make a suggestion with a clear instruction?

Friday · Clay faces

Resources	Access to trees, clay, jug of water, other natural materials.
Intent	To use talk to make descriptions, to engage in conversations, to learn new vocabulary.
Implement	Make clay faces to stick onto trees. Other natural items could be added for features such as small stones, sticks, feathers, moss, grass, etc. Encourage conversations about clay faces. Ask children what do you think will happen now that we have put our clay faces here?
Impact	Can children describe or talk about the features on their clay face?

Week 11

Monday · Find the bear outside

Resources	Teddy Bear.
Intent	Develop listening skills, develop pronunciation, take turns, understand why questions, use longer sentences.
Implement	One child is taken aside while a teddy bear is hidden somewhere in the garden. Tell the other children they are going to guide the child to the teddy by singing louder as the child gets closer to, or quietly as the child moves further away from the teddy until the child finds the Teddy, take turns to find the bear. Is it harder to hear outside?
Impact	Did children sing high and low to guide the child who was looking for the bear? Do children understand short sentences?

Tuesday · Giant Noughts and Crosses	
Resources	Twigs/sticks, stones, tape.
Intent	To take turns, to use talk to work out problems and organise thinking and activities.
Implement	Play noughts and crosses. Create a large 3x3 square or grid outside using tape. The twigs and stones can represent the noughts and crosses. Explain to children that they need to take turns to add one item in a box, one child will have twigs and the other stones and the idea is to get three objects in a row to win. Each player must take a turn each.
Impact	Can children work with others to solve a problem?

Wednesday · Chalk maze	
Resources	Chalk.
Intent	To listen and respond to others, to make suggestions and ideas.
Implement	Make a chalk maze for the children to follow the path. Chalks can be then left out to encourage children to do the same for each other.
Impact	Can children make suggestions? Can children listen and respond to others' ideas?

Thursday · Egg surprises	
Resources	Pre-filled plastic eggs filled with different items that make sounds such as rice, bell, lentils etc. sealed up.
Intent	Develop listening skills, distinguish between different sounds, use a wide range of vocabulary, understand why questions, use longer sentences, represent a point of view, hold a conversation.
Implement	Put an object inside a plastic hollow egg such as rice, bell etc. seal the eggs, pass around and shake. Listen carefully. Can the children work out what is in the egg? Why do you think it's a …?
Impact	Can children hear different sounds? Can children answer a why question?

Friday · The longest stick	
Resources	Sticks outside.
Intent	To be able to express a point of view, to continue a conversation with another.
Implement	Ask children to find the longest stick outside and compare and measure. Can you make a picture with your sticks?
Impact	Can children talk about what they have found and give reasons? Can children talk about similarities and differences?

Week 12

Monday · Which Superhero are you?	
Resources	Superhero mask templates, collage materials, pens, pencils, glue, tape, sequins etc.
Intent	Use talk to organise themselves and their play, to use imaginative language for role play, to initiate conversations?
Implement	Children can create their own superhero masks and talk about their 'character' with another. They can then play and act out their superhero. What materials have you chosen and why? Who will you be? What superpowers will you have?
Impact	Can children talk about the materials they used? Can children talk about who their imaginary character is?

Tuesday · It's a wrap!	
Resources	Books, tape, wrapping paper, scissors.
Intent	To make predictions, to discuss features and own experiences, to enjoy listening to stories with another.
Implement	Wrap up a mystery story to read at group time. Ask children to predict what it might be. Encourage children to wrap up a book for a friend to surprise them and share together. Why did they choose that book?
Impact	Can children make a prediction? Can children say why they chose a particular book? Can children share a book with another?

Wednesday · Leaf hunt	
Resources	Leaves.
Intent	To use a wider range of vocabulary, to join in with repetitive parts to a chant, to make suggestions.
Implement	Chant 'We're going on a leaf hunt; we're going to find a big one what a beautiful day'… add more parts to the chant if you wish. Change a leaf focus each time, such as 'a yellow one',' a small one', 'a broken one' etc).
Impact	Can children add a new word to the chant? Can children join in with the repetitive parts to the chant?

Thursday · Nature necklaces	
Resources	String, ribbon, natural materials (e.g. dried flowers, leaves).
Intent	To understand why questions, to hold a conversation for several turns, to express a point of view.
Implement	We are going to make nature necklaces. Give each child some ribbon, or even better discover it hanging on a tree and add leaves and flowers to it to make a necklace. Encourage children to talk about their choices during the making of the necklaces. Discuss design and if they wish to make adaptations.

Impact	Can children discuss their designs and why they chose the materials they did? Can children articulate what changes they could make?
Friday - What's the story?	
Resources	Collection of pictures of well-known stories, books to match.
Intent	To ask questions to find out more, to describe events in stories, to articulate their ideas and thoughts in well-formed sentences, to answer and understand why questions, to talk about familiar books.
Implement	Scatter the books in the middle of the group. Hold up an image from one of the stories. Children must match the image to the book and give reasons why they think it belongs to that book. Which character is this from? Why does this picture go with this book? Who can remember what happens next?
Impact	Can children give explanations to their answers? Can children form longer sentences? Can children match the image to the correct book?

Week 13

Monday · Story stones	
Resources	Stones, pens or paints, bag, (could use stickers if time is limited).
Intent	To continue a story, to use longer sentences, to develop listening skills.
Implement	Each child can draw, paint an image onto a stone. Wait for the stones to dry and add them to a bag. Take each one out and lay them in a circle. Adult can then model telling a story using the stone images as prompts, then children can add parts to the story from their decorated stone.
Impact	Can children listen to a story? Can children continue a story?

Tuesday · Nature monster	
Resources	Natural materials e.g., grass, leaves, dried flowers, twigs, stones, mud etc).
Intent	To start a conversation with an adult and continue it for many turns, to begin to make up own stories.
Implement	Create a nature monster out of natural materials. Talk with the children about what materials they would like to use for the features. Follow up ideas – create a story using the monster, or story stones from yesterday.
Impact	Can children talk about the features of their monster? Can children make up their own story?

Wednesday – Make up a story	
Resources	None.
Intent	To articulate their ideas and thoughts in well-formed sentences, to develop listening skills, to express a point of view, use story language and develop imagination.
Implement	Children to sit in a circle around a stage which can just make out. Invite a child to start a story. Help the child to think about their character, what or who are they going to be? What are they going to do? Who might be another character in the story, would they like to come up to the 'stage', what will that character do? Children can take turns to tell a story and others can contribute along the way.
Impact	Can children think of a part of a story? Can children act out a character?

Thursday · Paint a mud picture	
Resources	Paintbrushes, paper, puddles or pots of water.
Intent	To use a wide range of vocabulary, to start a conversation with an adult, to describe their creations with some detail.
Implement	Encourage children to paint using mud and talk about their creations. Can they add anything from the environment to their art? Ask children about their creation or ask them to talk about it with their friends.

Impact	Can children describe their mud picture to you? Can children hold a conversation, taking it in turns to speak?
Friday · Magic wands	
Resources	Sticks, feathers, wool/string or ribbon, grass, other natural materials, story about magic.
Intent	To use a wider range of vocabulary, to use longer sentences, to use talk to organise themselves and their play.
Implement	Read a story to the children about magic. Ask children to create 'magic' wands using natural materials. Ask the children to cast a 'spell'.
Impact	Can children use longer sentences to 'cast a spell'?

Week 14

Monday · Singing snowball	
Resources	Recycled newspaper or scrap paper, recycling bin, nursery rhymes on card/images, feely bag.
Intent	To sing a large repertoire of songs, to join in with familiar songs and rhymes.
Implement	Give each child a piece of paper to scrunch into a ball. The aim is to throw the 'snowball' into the bin. Each time it lands in the bin we all sing a nursery rhyme/song together. These can be on cards for the adult (or child) to choose from a feely bag. Which song shall we pick? I wonder which song will be chosen next..?
Impact	Can children join in with familiar songs/rhymes?
Tuesday · Find the golden nuggets	
Resources	Pre-made 'golden nuggets' (stones or pebbles painted gold), paper, pencils/pens, treasure box.
Intent	To ask questions to find out more and to check they understand what has been said to them, to take turns in conversations.
Implement	Hide the 'treasure' outside and make a treasure map for the children to locate the golden nuggets. This could be adapted to scatter the nuggets in different places or put them all in one location in a box. Children can then have a go at taking turns to hide and create maps for others to find.
Impact	Can children find the 'treasure' by communicating with others? Can children ask questions to find out more and check their understanding?
Wednesday · Rhyming odd one out	
Resources	3 objects or pictures, 2 with names that rhyme and 1 with a name that does not.
Intent	To identify rhyme, to use longer sentences, to explain their answers.

Implement	Ask the children to identify the 'odd one out' by looking at the pictures. What do they think could be different about one of them? You may need to model first. Ask children to say out loud what they are, can they see now which is the off one out and why. The name that does not rhyme. Spend time looking and talking about the objects.
Impact	Can children identify the odd rhyme out? Can children talk about why they think something is the odd one out?

Thursday · What plant am I?	
Resources	Variety of commonly known small plants or herbs.
Intent	To describe features of an object, to develop listening skills.
Implement	Make sure children know the names of the plants chosen beforehand or number the plants. Have them laid out in front of the group. Talk about the features of one of the plants. Children have to guess which one you were thinking of, they can point to it. Children then have a turn describing without naming for others to guess.
Impact	Can children listen to another's description? Cam children guess what plant they are talking about?

Friday · Leaf whispers	
Resources	A leaf.
Intent	To understand how to listen carefully and why listening is important.
Implement	Everyone sits in a circle. An adult whispers a word or simple sentence to a child and hands them the leaf. The child with the leaf then repeats the message to the next child, then passes them the leaf. The game ends when the leaf has returned to the start and the last person states the message. Talk about how the message changed/did it stay the same? Repeat with other children or another adult starting.
Impact	Can children repeat back a message?

Week 15

Monday · Nursery rhyme mash up	
Resources	None needed, or Nursery Rhyme picture cards to prompt.
Intent	To notice similarities and differences, to identify rhyme, to join in with familiar nursery rhymes.
Implement	Sing different versions of Nursery rhymes. Can children work out the mistakes and correct you, for example 'Baa, Baa Black Sheep sat on the wall', 'Humpty Dumpty went up the hill to fetch a pail of water…'
Impact	Can children spot the different word or phrase in the familiar nursery rhyme? Can children join in with familiar nursery rhymes?

Tuesday · Stick Man/Woman	

Resources	Sticks, feathers, grass, other natural materials, googly eyes (if wish).
Intent	To retell or make up a story, to use longer sentences.
Implement	Create a 'stick man or woman' and talk about the features and materials chosen. Use these to tell a story. It could be Stick Man, The Gingerbread Man, or a new made-up story.
Impact	Can children recall parts of a story? Can children use longer sentences to make up their own story?

Wednesday · The duplication game

Resources	Basketful of natural resources approximately 6 different (a feather, a pine cone, a pebble, a leaf, acorn etc).
Intent	To listen to an instruction, to follow an instruction.
Implement	Go outside. Pull an item out of the basket and ask the children to find that item and match it. Repeat with the next item. How do you know it was a match?
Impact	Can children listen to an instruction? Can children find a matching item?

Thursday · Construct a labyrinth

Resources	Variety of sticks.
Intent	To use talk to help work out problems and organise thinking and activities.
Implement	Using sticks lay out a maze outside for children to follow. Something could be at the end of it for example ,can they find their way to Teddy?
Impact	Can children solve a problem by talking to others?

Friday · Puppet theatre

Resources	Puppets, or stick people from earlier in week, box or crates, material.
Intent	To use talk to help work out problems and organise thinking and activities, to use imaginative talk in their play.
Implement	Children can help make a puppet theatre so they can put on 'a show' for others. Can be inside or outside. You will need to model a puppet show beforehand but once children see how to do it they will enjoy putting on a show for hours!
Impact	Can children use imaginative language in role play?

Week 16

Monday · Matching pairs	
Resources	6 paired objects e.g. 2 pebbles, 2 shells, 2 counters, etc), 12 paper plates.
Intent	To use talk to help work out problems and organise thinking and activities, to take turns in conversation.
Implement	Set out paper plates (3 rows of 4) and hide each item under a different plate. Children take turns to turn over 2 plates and see if they have a matching pair.
Impact	Can children work with others communicating ideas? Can children work together to find a matching pair?

Tuesday · Traffic lights	
Resources	None needed.
Intent	To develop listening skills, to understand and respond to commands and actions.
Implement	Children run around and when you shout 'red' they stop, 'amber' they walk and 'green' they run.
Impact	Can children carry out the correct action to match the command?

Wednesday · Sausages	
Resources	Story book.
Intent	To develop listening skills, to talk about familiar books, to listen to familiar stories and identify particular words in those stories.
Implement	Choose one of the children's favourite stories and select a word that appears with reasonable frequency, for example the name of the main character. Explain that they need to listen for the word and each time they hear it they need to shout sausages.
Impact	Can children identify the chosen words? Can children respond appropriately to the 'rule' of the game?

Thursday · Nature memory game	
Resources	Up to 7 natural objects (e.g. pine cone, shell, leaf, twig, flower, pebble, clump of moss), tray, material to cover.
Intent	To develop recall of objects, to be able to say when there is a difference.
Implement	Show children all the items on the tray. Ask them to have a good look at them. Cover with a piece of material and secretly take one away. Reveal the items on the tray. Which item has disappeared? Repeat several times.
Impact	Can children remember the items on the tray? Can children say the item that has disappeared on the tray?

Friday · Musical noises	

Resources	On laminated cards have symbols/pictures or words that show 1. a musical note with an open mouth, 2. the words La la, 3. the word hum with a mouth closed.
Intent	To discover new ways to sing familiar songs, to make noises to the tune of the song, to follow instructions.
Implement	Show the children the different cards and explain what they mean. Select a chosen familiar nursery rhyme. Mix up the cards - pull out one at random. Everyone has to either hum the chosen song, sing the chosen song normally or say la la to the tune for the chosen song.
Impact	Can children join in with a familiar song, singing it in different ways?

Week 17

Monday - Spiderman

Resources	Instruments.
Intent	To respond to different sounds and actions.
Implement	'Spiderman' has a range of instruments, and the children decide what movement goes with which sound (e.g. shakers for running on tiptoe, triangle for fairy steps). First an adult will need to model being Spiderman. Then a child takes the role. Spiderman stands with his back to the others and plays an instrument. The other children move towards Spiderman in the manner of the instrument while it is playing. They stop when it stops. The first person to reach Spiderman takes over that role and the game starts again.
Impact	Can children make different actions to different sounds?

Tuesday - Musical statues with a twist

Resources	Music.
Intent	To listen carefully and respond with actions.
Implement	Play their favourite music, ask children to clap and dance to the music listening to the beat, when the music stops, strike a pose and freeze. As a variation, ask children to take turns to play the music with instruments.
Impact	Can children stop immediately when the music stops? Can children respond to music in different ways?

Wednesday - Laundry

Resources	Range of clothes, socks.
Intent	To develop vocabulary, to follow instructions.
Implement	Place a range of matching clothes and socks in the middle of the room. The children have to find the matching pairs of socks or sort the clothes into the same colours depending on the instructions given. Repeat several times with different ways to sort. Can you put all the pink items together? Can you find all the matching socks, can you fold all of the trousers into a pile etc?

Impact	Can children sort the items of clothing according to the instructions given?
Thursday · Rhyming book	
Resources	A rhyming book.
Intent	To join in with rhyming words from a story, to identify a rhyming word, to suggest a rhyming word.
Implement	Share a rhyming book with the group. Children identify the rhyming words throughout the story. Can they think of other words that rhyme?
Impact	Can children identify a rhyming word? Can children suggest a rhyming word?
Friday · Mud pizzas	
Resources	Mud, mud kitchen if have, trays, natural materials, leaves, herbs, water.
Intent	To engage with others in conversation, to share ideas with others, to pay attention to more than one thing at a time.
Implement	Making mud pizzas! Talk about what 'toppings' the children want for their 'mud pizzas'. What else could they add? Talk about how they made them. Share their 'recipe' with a friend.
Impact	Can children discuss their ideas with another person?

Week 18

Monday · Making stories	
Resources	Different loose parts, dried flowers, corks, sticks, various fabrics etc.
Intent	Engage in extended conversations about stories, to develop stories and use imaginative vocabulary.
Implement	Give the children a variety of loose parts and model making different things out of them for example a person with the cork and use the flowers for faces etc. then model creating a scene, for example a river with some fabric and make up a story with the little person.
Impact	Can children use story language? Can children create a simple story using props?
Tuesday · Name the toy	
Resources	Variety of toys for example, a doll, spider, dinosaur, goat, cow, pig, hedgehog.
Intent	To develop a narrative in their play, to listen carefully to the initial sound in words and find the same.
Implement	Ask the children to give toys names that begin with the same sound as the item such as Daisy doll, Sammy spider etc. show the children how to play with them after in the small world.

Impact	Can children think of a name with the same initial sound as the toy? Can children create a narrative using toys and/or props?
Wednesday · I hear with my little ear...	
Resources	None needed.
Intent	To distinguish between sounds, to listen for sounds in the environment.
Implement	Play this game outside and children listen for sounds. What sounds can we hear? ...something that sounds like (make the sound) or begins with.
Impact	Can children tell you what they can hear?
Thursday · Nature paint brushes	
Resources	Sticks, leylandii leaves/feathers/sprigs of herbs (what is available), tape/elastic bands/wool/string, paint or mud, paper.
Intent	To start a conversation with an adult and continue it for many turns, to use and apply new vocabulary.
Implement	Attach natural materials to a stick using tape/elastic bands or string and children can paint a picture using paint or mud. Encourage children to talk about the materials selected and the image they made. Talk about the techniques/effects the materials produced (e.g. wavy, smooth, rough, patchy).
Impact	Can children talk about their paintbrush using a range of new vocabulary?
Friday · Body percussion	
Resources	None needed.
Intent	To copy sounds and actions, to understand how to listen carefully and why listening is important.
Implement	What sounds can we make with our hands? Children think of different sounds their hands can make. Choose children to make a sound and others to copy, for example, gentle taps with 1 or 2, fingers, clicks, pats, rub around in circles etc.
Impact	Can children copy sounds and actions?

Week 19

Monday · Aliens	
Resources	Alien.
Intent	To recognise words with the same initial sound (alliteration).
Implement	Introduce your alien, he is called Boo Boz Bop. What is your alien's name - it has to start with the sound of your real name? Go around and ask each child. If children would rather not tell, you can make up their name for them or ask the alien to!

Impact	Can children hear the initial sound in a name? Can children sound out the initial sound in a name? Can children think of a matching initial sound in a name?
Tuesday · Buried Treasure	
Resources	Toy cat or image, image of a bin, image of a treasure chest, 4 images or items that rhyme with cat, 4 images or items that do not rhyme with cat.
Intent	To identify a rhyming word, to suggest a rhyming word.
Implement	We are going to bury some treasure! Display the items and look at each item one at a time and decide if it rhymes with 'cat' and put it in the treasure chest.
Impact	Can children identify a rhyming word? Can children suggest a rhyming word? Can children say which word does not rhyme?
Wednesday · Scented water play	
Resources	Water tray, sliced oranges, sliced lemons, sliced cucumbers, mint leaves, containers/pots, spoons.
Intent	To learn new vocabulary, to answer simple questions, to understand 'why' questions.
Implement	Talk about the scents in the water. What can you smell? Describe the smell? What reminds you of that smell? Sweet, strong, fresh etc.
Impact	Can children talk about objects using their senses? Can children answer simple questions?
Thursday · Large scale train	
Resources	Blocks, boxes, crates, chairs, paper for tickets.
Intent	To talk about own experiences, to use a wider range of vocabulary, to start a conversation with an adult or friend, to use talk to organise their play.
Implement	Make a large train with the children to go on a 'journey', get on and off, take turns to be the 'driver' and 'ticket collector'. Talk about where to go, real life journeys they have been on.
Impact	Can children share with others about their own experiences? Can children use talk to organise their play?
Friday · What's missing?	
Resources	Leaf, sheep, soap, fish, sock, bus, blanket.
Intent	To pay attention to more than one thing at a time, to identify different sounds in words, to blend sounds into words.
Implement	Lay out a selection of familiar objects with names that contain three phonemes, for example, leaf, sheep, soap, fish, sock, bus.. Check that all the children can recognise each object. Put a blanket over the top ask children to close their eyes while singing 'hide them hide them what is hiding here' and sneak an object out. Take off the blanket, which is missing? Can you sound talk it? Use robot arms to help you. Repeat.

| Impact | Can children talk about what item is missing? Can children identify different sounds in words? Can children make attempts to blend sounds into words? |

Week 20

Monday - Journey Stick	
Resources	Sticks, clear tape or double sided
Intent	To recall an event, to talk about what they see using a wide variety of vocabulary.
Implement	Take your stick outside (could be somewhere other than the outside area) and as you walk collect items along the way to attach to your stick to then recall your journey and discoveries once back inside.

Impact	Can children recall their journey using the materials from their journey stick as a reminder?

Tuesday · Large scale bus

Resources	Blocks, boxes, crates, chairs, paper for tickets, pretend money.
Intent	To talk about own experiences, to use a wider range of vocabulary, to start a conversation with an adult or friend, to use talk to organise their play.
Implement	Make a large bus with the children to go on a 'journey', get on and off, take turns to be the 'driver'. Talk about where to go, fares, real life journeys they have been on etc. Talk about bus stops along the way.
Impact	Can children share with others about their own experiences? Can children use talk to organise their play?

Wednesday · Buried Treasure

Resources	Toy hen or image, image of a bin, image of a treasure chest, 4 images or items that rhyme with hen, 4 images or items that do not rhyme with hen.
Intent	To identify a rhyming word, to suggest a rhyming word.
Implement	We are going to bury some treasure! Display the different items. Look at each item one at a time and decide if it rhymes with 'hen' put it in the treasure chest. If not, it goes on the bin card.
Impact	Can children identify a rhyming word? Can children suggest a rhyming word? Can children say when a word does not rhyme?

Thursday – Put the spider on the web

Resources	Web drawn onto paper, toy spiders, blindfold.
Intent	To listen carefully and respond with actions.
Implement	Sing Incy Wincy spider. We are going to play a game! The children need to put the spider in the centre of the web with a blindfold on! Children can take turns to wear the blindfold on and put the spider on the web. Take off the blindfold and see if you got it in the middle!
Impact	Can children take turns? Can children use a wider vocabulary?

Friday – Bug hunt!

Resources	Bug cards, magnifying glasses, outside space.
Intent	Extend vocabulary, talk about similarities and differences.
Implement	Show children the bug pictures and tell them we are going to see if we can find them! Talk about the colours of the bugs and what is different about them for example a ladybird is red and has spots. Ask lots of questions while the children are exploring.

| Impact | Can children talk about the bugs?
Can children talk about the different features of the bugs?
Can children answer questions? |

For planning, resources and training please visit:

www.earlyyearsstaffroom.com

© Early Years Staffroom.com Ltd